A Glance at History in the Everglades Area *of Florida*

Marya Repko

ECITY • PUBLISHING

A Glance at History in the Everglades Area of Florida

© 2020 text by Marya Repko
All rights reserved.

cover sketch of Everglades City Hall courtesy of Matthew Goldman (constantwaterman.com))
Historic photographs in this book are from the Florida State Archives unless otherwise noted.

set in Century Schoolbook, 12/16pt
printed & bound in the USA
First Edition, First Printing, March 2020

ABOUT THE TYPE FACE
The Century family of type was designed for Century Publishing in 1894 by typographer Linn Boyd Benton of American Type Founders and revised by his son Morris Fuller Benton. "Century Schoolbook" was commissioned in 1919 by textbook publisher Ginn & Co. and is known for its legibility.

ISBN 978-1-7341046-0-8

ECITY • PUBLISHING

P O Box 5033
Everglades City, FL, 34139
telephone (239) 695-2905
www.ecity-publishing.com

Other books from this publisher:
   A Brief History of the Everglades City Area
   The Story of Everglades City; A History for Younger Readers
   Historia de Everglades City (Spanish translation by Gloria Gutiérrez)
   A Brief History of the Fakahatchee
   A Brief History of Sanibel Island
   The Story of Sanibel Island; A History for Younger Readers
   Angel of the Swamp; Deaconess Harriet Bedell in the Everglades
   Grandma of the Glades; A Brief Biography of Marjory Stoneman Douglas
   Memories from Hadlyme; A Personal History of the East Haddam, CT, Area
   Women in the Everglades; Pioneers and Early Environmentalists
   The Story of Barron Collier; A History for Younger Readers
   Everglades Entrepreneur; Barron Gift Collier, Roaring Twenties Tycoon

A Glance at History in the Everglades Area

PREFACE

This book was written after the opening of the Everglades Area Visitor Center on February 1, 2020. I hope it will answer some of the questions posed by tourists new to our unique environment and heritage.

The proceeds will be donated to benefit the Center.

Marya Repko
Everglades City, FL
mrepko@earthlink.net
February, 2020

A Glance at History in the Everglades Area

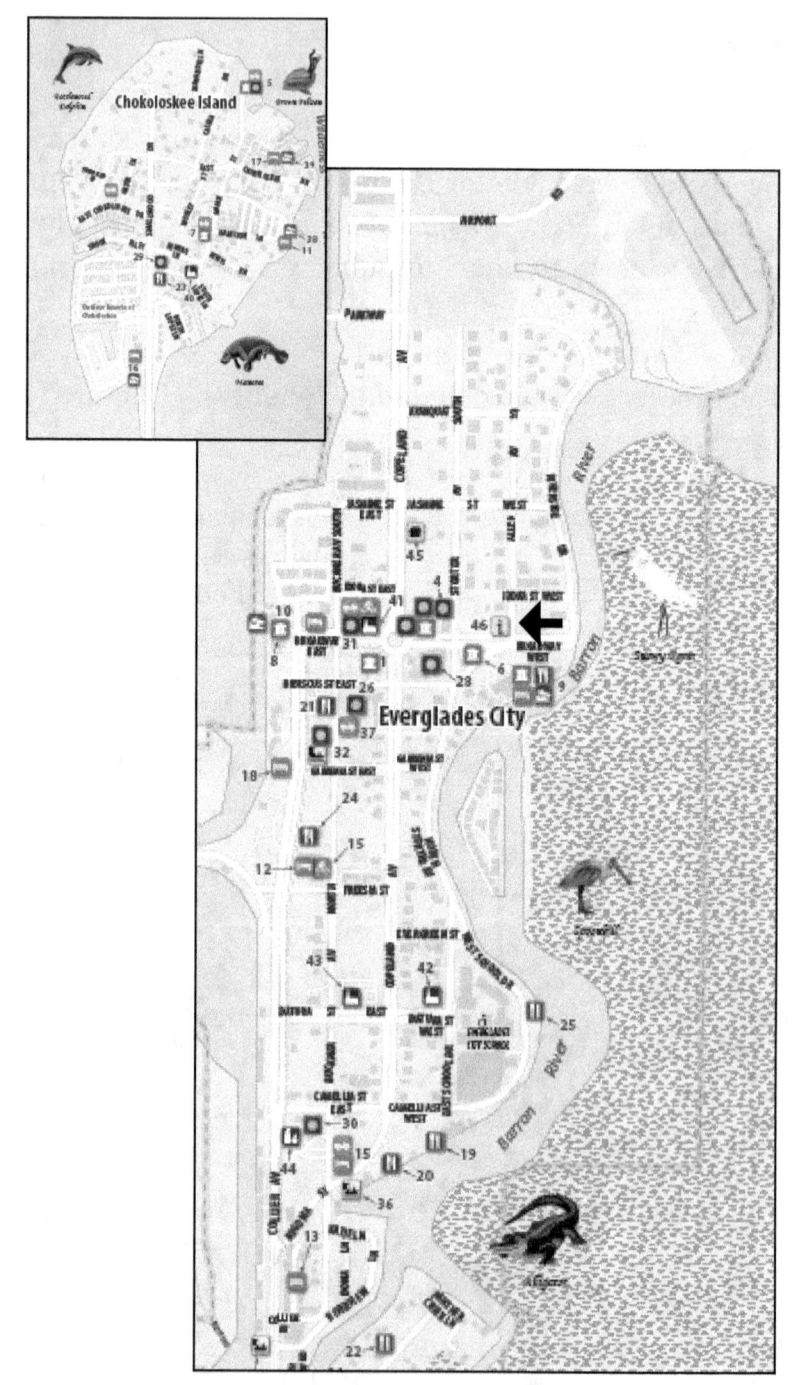

A Glance at History in the Everglades Area

CONTENTS

EARLY TIMES, 1513-1860s 1

PIONEERS, 1870s-1920s 3

COUNTY & TRAIL, 1923-1928 5

SEMINOLES & DEACONESS, 1933-1960 9

TOMATOES & LOGGING, 1928-1957 11

DRAINAGE & CONSERVATION, 1901-1967 15

EVERGLADES CITY, 1953-now 17

HURRICANES, 1910-2017 19

DEVELOPMENT, 1950s-now 21

FURTHER READING 24

TIMELINE 25

A Glance at History in the Everglades Area

Florida in 1859. The Everglades area was in Monroe County whose seat was Key West. In 1887 Lee County was established and in 1923 Collier County was formed. The newer counties included the village of Everglade.

A Glance at History in the Everglades Area

EARLY TIMES, 1513-1860s

When the Spanish explored the Southwest coast of Florida in the early 1500s, they found a tribe of Native Americans known as the Calusa. These inhabitants ate the seafood they caught in the Gulf waters. They built shell mounds to keep themselves high and dry during floods.

The Calusa were large people and seemed like giants to the Spanish who are not very tall. The tribe and the new Europeans fought when the Spanish tried to convert the Calusa to a new religion. Other Calusa died of foreign diseases (e.g., influenza) that the Spanish brought.

In 1763, Florida became British after a European treaty and the Spanish moved to Cuba. Most of the Calusa went with them.

In 1821, the United States acquired the Territory of Florida. At this time, the American government was trying to move Natives out of the southern states of Georgia and Alabama to make the land free for white farmers. The tribes, known as the Seminoles, moved south into Florida where they fought with the U. S. Army. Eventually, in 1857, a few Seminoles settled in the Everglades where the Army could not follow them.

A Glance at History in the Everglades Area

Florida was made a State in 1845. During the Civil War between the North and the South (1861-1866), the biggest city in south Florida was the shipping port of Key West. It was the seat of Monroe County which included most of the Everglades area.

When the Spanish arrived in Southwest Florida during the early 1500s, they found a tribe called the Calusa. This little wooden idol carved by them is on display at the Marco Island Museum of History.

A Glance at History in the Everglades Area

PIONEERS, 1870s-1920s

Settlers came to the western Everglades after the Civil War ended in 1866. They had to travel by boat because there were no roads in this area. They were looking for a frost-free climate to grow crops and for land where they could live.

The first permanent settler on the little "Potato Creek" river in Everglade was William Smith Allen from Key West. He had grown castor beans in Sanibel until a hurricane destroyed his crop. On his sail home, he discovered John Weeks farming on the river bank.

In 1889, Allen sold out to the Storter family who enlarged the home on the river and opened a trading post. The family grew sugar cane which they reduced to syrup and took by sailboat to Key West to sell. They also offered lodging to visiting anglers. The Post Office called "Everglade" was established in 1893. The Storter home is now the famous Rod & Gun Lodge.

The other local families (e.g., Hamilton, Daniels, Weeks, Brown) grew vegetables, such as tomatoes and cucumbers, that they sold in the market at Key West. They also fished for mullet that they salted and packed in barrels to sell. On their return from Key West, they brought their mail and supplies. The

A Glance at History in the Everglades Area

pioneers were very independent and used home remedies when they got sick.

On the island of Chokoloskee, a Post Office was established in 1891 by C. G. McKinney, called "the sage of Chokoloskee". Ted Smallwood became postmaster in 1906 and opened a trading post where he dealt with the Seminoles. He learned their language and they trusted him to buy their skins or deer meat.

The Storter homestead and store on the river in Everglade (above) and Ted Smallwood outside his trading post in Chokoloskee (bottom).

A Glance at History in the Everglades Area

COUNTY & TRAIL, 1923-1928

The Everglades area pioneers continued to be hardy and self-sufficient until the early 1920s. Their lives changed when a man named Barron Gift Collier arrived.

Collier was born in Memphis, Tennessee, in 1873. He made a fortune selling streetcar advertising and became an important figure in New York during the "roaring twenties". He discovered Florida in 1911 when he visited the little island of Useppa (west of Fort Myers) which he bought and made his Florida residence.

Collier then bought the grapefruit farm in Deep Lake, about 15 miles north of the village of Everglade in 1921. He thought he could develop this area and added more land until he owned over a million acres.

But, there was no road. The "Tamiami Trail" (Tampa to Miami) was started in 1914 but it only went to Naples on the west coast and as far as the Dade County line on the east coast. No one wanted to build the road to join them through the swamp. Collier promised to finish the road if his land were made into a new county. In 1923, Collier County was established by the Florida legislature. It is still the largest county in Florida.

A Glance at History in the Everglades Area

Collier selected the village of Everglade as his County seat and engineering headquarters because it had a navigable river which he named "Barron" after himself. He hired David Graham Copeland, a naval engineer, to supervise the projects. They built a little city called "Everglades" and completed the road in only five years. There was a big celebration on April 26, 1928, when cars drove into the new city for the official opening of the new Trail.

Building the Trail (now US-41) was a difficult task. It was all overgrown and swampy. When the dredges moved soil to pile up on the roadbed, they discovered limestone under the mud. Many tons of dynamite were used to break up the rock. Workers, mostly African-Americans from Georgia, slept and ate in mobile homes that followed the construction. If they got sick from "muck poisoning" they were treated in the little Juliet Carnes Collier hospital in Everglades, named after Barron's wife.

Barron Collier (center) bought land in Southwest Florida in the early 1920s. He is seen here on the little rail car that carried citrus fruit from the farm in Deep Lake to the river in Everglades where it was loaded onto ships going to market. *photo courtesy Collier County Museum, Naples, FL*

A Glance at History in the Everglades Area

Downtown Everglades in 1928 after it was built in the Florida wilderness. Some of the historic buildings are the County Courthouse (now Everglades City Hall) and the Atlantic Coast Line railroad Depot. *photos courtesy Collier County Museum, Naples, FL*

A Glance at History in the Everglades Area

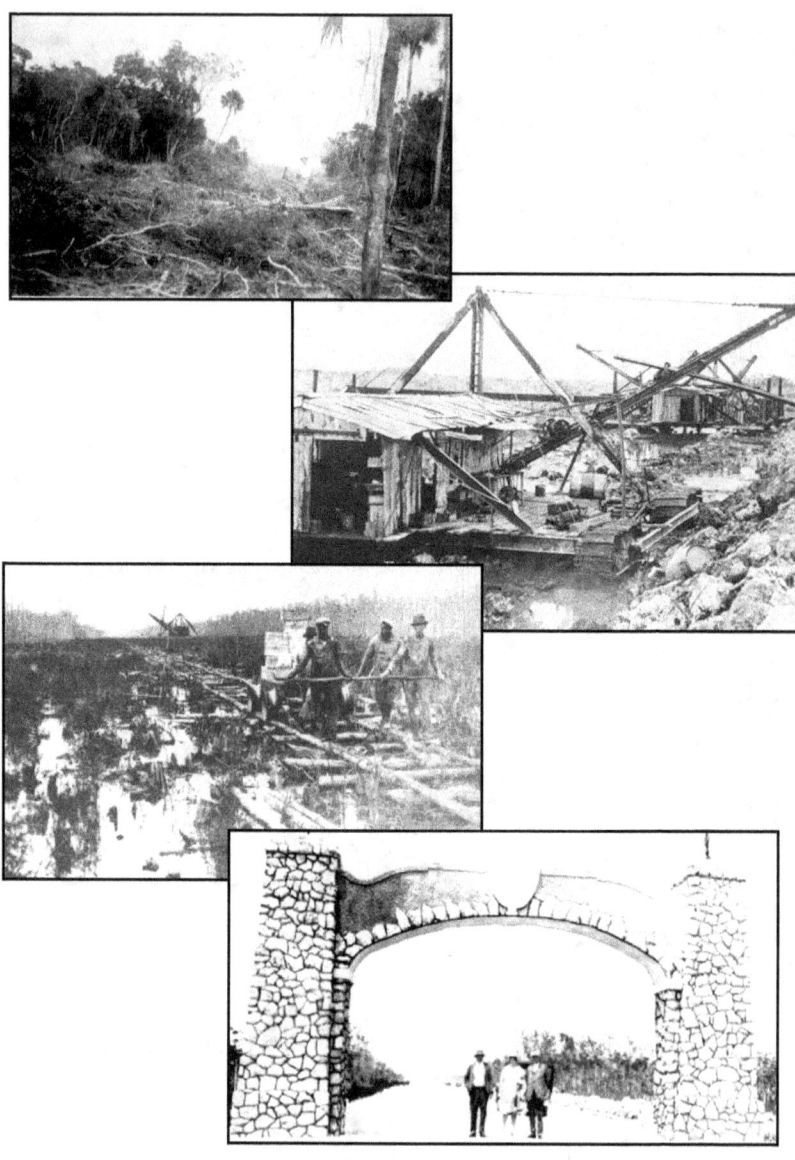

Building the Tamiami Trail involved cutting a path through the jungle, dredging up fill for the road bed, using tons of dynamite to break up the limestone under the muck, and eventually smoothing out gravel for a road. The arch marked the Dade and Collier County boundary. *photos courtesy Collier County Museum, Naples, FL*

A Glance at History in the Everglades Area

SEMINOLES & DEACONESS, 1933

The canal next to the Tamiami Trail, which runs east/west, drained the water that the Seminoles had canoed to their traditional hunting grounds to the north. To earn money, they built little "Indian Villages" where they sold souvenirs and performed "gator wrestling" stunts for the tourists on the Trail.

In the early 1930s, Deaconess Harriet Bedell found them when she was raising funds for the Episcopal Missions. She was born in Buffalo, New York, in 1875 and worked with Native Americans in Oklahoma and Alaska. When she saw how miserable the Seminoles were, she convinced the bishop to let her open a mission in Everglades. She encouraged the Seminoles to bring their patchwork clothing and baskets to sell. She drove her car to the big stores in Miami with their crafts and gave the Indians all the money to buy more supplies.

She also went out to their villages in remote areas to help them live a healthy life. She did not force them to join her religion and they respected her for that. When the medicine man in the tribe could not cure a European disease like influenza, he asked the Deaconess for help. She gave them aspirin and chicken soup.

A Glance at History in the Everglades Area

She was also loved by her neighbors in Everglades and taught Sunday School on nearby Marco Island. There is a chapel dedicated to Deaconess Bedell there in Saint Mark's Episcopal Church.

After Hurricane Donna in 1960, the Deaconess moved to a retirement home where she volunteered until she died aged 93 in 1969. The Episcopal Church added her name to its list of Lesser Feasts and Fasts in 2009, a way of recognizing the good works she did during her life.

Deaconess Harriet Bedell lived in Everglades from 1933 to 1960 in a little house on Camellia Street. She helped the Seminoles to sell their patchwork clothing and visited them in their remote villages.

A Glance at History in the Everglades Area

TOMATOES & LOGGING, 1928

The Tamiami Trail opened up the area to industry. James Gaunt bought land around the village he called "Ochopee" (big farm) and planted acres of tomatoes. Hundreds of people were employed in the fields and the packing plant. There was a Post Office, general store, and lodging house for travelers as well as homes for workers.

In 1953, a fire burned down the store. Gaunt moved a little shed to sort the mail. It is now known as the smallest Post Office in the United States. The delivery route is over 100 miles. The little building is a tourist attraction and postcards can be sent with a special stamp.

The land eventually became poor from changes in the environment and the tomato farming was moved to Immokalee (40 miles north).

There were also tomato fields in the village of Copeland, about 3 miles north of the Tamiami Trail on SR-29. This venture was started by the Janes brothers and Carl Webb. Besides the Janes Restaurant and store in Copeland, they established the WinCar Hardware store in Everglades which still exists today.

A Glance at History in the Everglades Area

The train line went from the Depot in Everglades north to Immokalee. The tomato harvest was carried by freight car to markets. The train line was closed in the late-1950s.

Unfortunately, the Copeland Post Office and Janes store complex was bought by Big Cypress National Preserve and torn down in 2001.

In 1943, the Lee Tidewater Cypress Company started cutting down the large trees in the Fakahatchee, west of SR-29, and shipped the logs by train to the sawmill in northern Florida. The company built a village for workers, many of them African-American. At the same time, pine trees were harvested in a new village called Jerome on the east side of SR-29 where the Jones Lumber Company had a sawmill.

By the late 1950s, the trees had all been cut down and there was no more logging. The Fakahatchee Strand became a State Preserve in 1974 and can be visited today on Janes Scenic Drive.

The little Ochopee Post Office, said to be the smallest one in the United States, also served as a bus stop along the Tamiami Trail in the 1950s.

A Glance at History in the Everglades Area

The huge cypress trees were logged in the Fakahatchee from 1943 until the late 1950s. Rail track was laid on Janes Scenic Drive to bring the large logs out of the forest. You can get a glimpse of the old-growth trees on the Boardwalk off the Tamiami Trail (about 7 miles west of SR-29).

A Glance at History in the Everglades Area

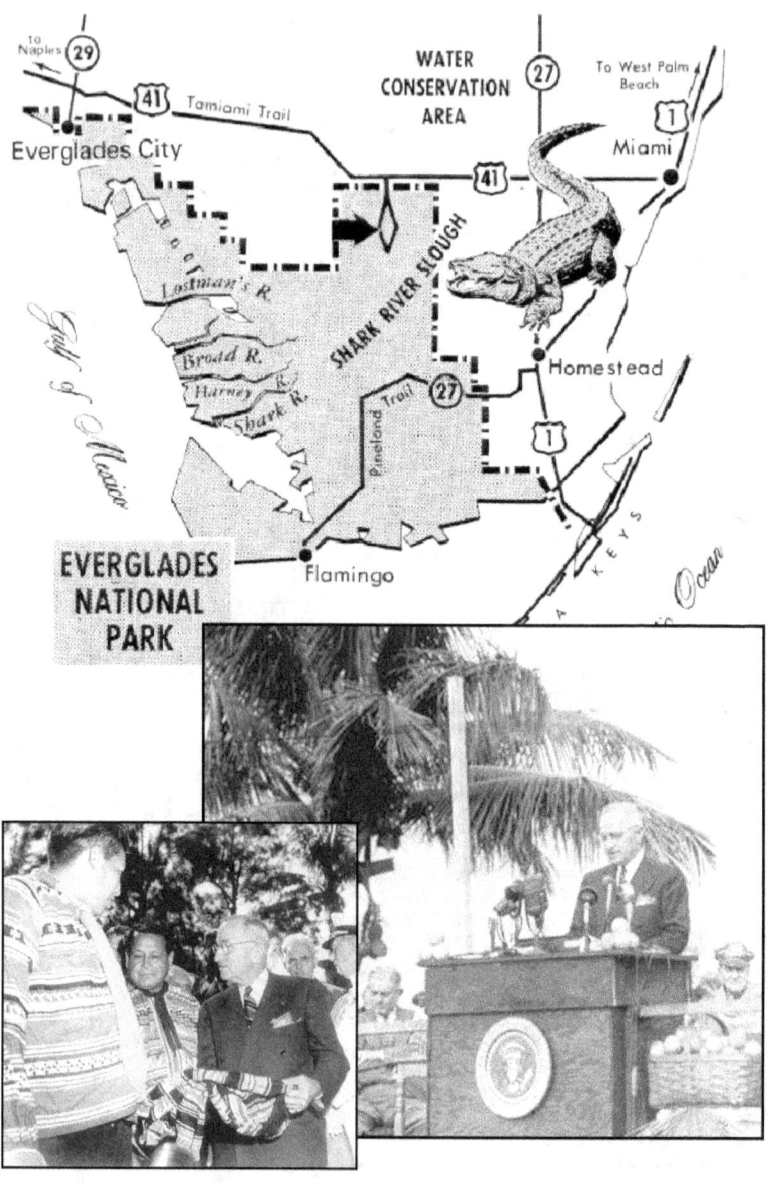

Everglades National Park was opened on December 6, 1947, by President Harry S Truman at a ceremony in Everglades. Local Seminoles presented him with a patchwork shirt.

A Glance at History in the Everglades Area

DRAINAGE & CONSERVATION

The State of Florida was granted the "Swamp and Overflowed Lands" in 1850 on condition that they were drained. It was thought to be a progressive move to recover land for agriculture. In the early 1900s, canals were built from Lake Okeechobee to the Atlantic coast. The Caloosahatchee River was widened to drain into the Gulf Coast.

Land was sold and farming started but, even with the drainage, there were floods during the summer rainy season. The towns of LaBelle, Clewiston, and Belle Meade grew up around the big lake. The land was suitable for sugar cane and there are still miles of cane fields there.

Further south, the Florida Federation of Women's Clubs established Royal Palm Hammock park in 1916 when they were given land by the widow of Henry Flagler, the railroad pioneer who developed Miami in 1896. This pristine wilderness became the nucleus of Everglades National Park which was officially opened on December 6, 1947, by President Harry S Truman at a ceremony in Everglades; Deaconess Harriet Bedell gave the invocation!

Just before the Park opened, Marjory Stoneman Douglas published her famous book *The Everglades; River of Grass*. She had lived in Miami writing for

A Glance at History in the Everglades Area

the "Herald" newspaper since 1915 and saw many changes in her long life until she died at age 108 in 1998. Her message was "water is the key".

She fought to stop a huge airport in the Big Cypress in 1967 that would hinder the flow of water into the Everglades. The Big Cypress National Preserve was established in 1974. After that, she tried to persuade the sugar farmers not to pollute Lake Okeechobee.

In 1947, Marjory Stoneman Douglas wrote her famous book. She gave speeches to fight the building of the Jetport in the Big Cypress in 1972 and was honored by Florida Governor Bob Graham in 1985. She was also given the Presidential Medal of Freedom in 1993 when she was 103 years old.

A Glance at History in the Everglades Area

EVERGLADES CITY, 1953 - now

Barron Collier died in 1939. The Collier Corporation began to move their operations to Naples which was growing because of its beaches and tourism. In 1953, the village of Everglades was incorporated into the City of Everglades. Many of the homes owned by the Collier Corporation were sold to the people who lived in them.

In 1959, a County referendum voted to relocate the County seat to East Naples. That was a green-field site and it was not until 1962 that the new Government Center was ready with a courthouse, jail, and offices. The old Courthouse building in Everglades was taken over as City offices but it still houses a branch of the County library and Tax Collector's office.

In 1923, Collier established the "Collier County News" newspaper (now the "Naples Daily News"), a telephone network (which eventually became part of Collier's Inter-County Telephone & Telegraph Company), and the Bank of Everglades (which moved to Immokalee in 1962).

Collier also owned a shipping line, a bus company, and a chain of luxury resort hotels in southern Florida including the Rod & Gun in Everglades which still welcomes visitors.

A Glance at History in the Everglades Area

The Mayor of Everglades from 1923 until 1959 was Daniel McLeod. He and his wife Lucy are honored in the park and recreation center for area children next to City Hall on the Circle. The famous Everglades Seafood Festival started as an event to raise money for the playground.

Collier built a commercial laundry to clean the sheets and towels from the Rod & Gun Lodge and the Everglades Inn. After World War II, the building was used as offices and then by the Everglades Women's Club who bought it. However, they could not repair the old wooden structure so the women got a grant from the State and gave the restored premises to the County. The Museum of the Everglades was opened on April 26, 1998, on the 70th Anniversary of the completion of the Tamiami Trail. The Friends of the Museum hold a Birthday Party every year.

A Glance at History in the Everglades Area

HURRICANES, 1910-2017

The first big storm that we know about was in 1910 when the Everglades schoolhouse floated away. After that, buildings were raised on pilings. The east coast storms in 1926 and 1935 did not have such a large impact here.

Most older residents remember Hurricane Donna on September 9, 1960. The water was so high that people took shelter on the second floor of the Courthouse. One man recalled that he swam across to the grocery store where the bread was floating around. You can see the high-water mark at Right Choice Supermarket inside the front door.

Although Hurricane Andrew in 1992 mainly hit the east coast, there was flooding here from storm surge. The next significant hurricane in this area was Wilma on October 24, 2005. It brought wind damage but not major flooding. After the hurricane, Everglades City Hall was completely restored with a grant from FEMA because of its historical importance.

Recently, we suffered from Hurricane Irma on September 9, 2017, which did cause flooding – not only water but slimy grey muck. The danger from mold was a problem if premises were not cleaned out and several historic buildings have been demolished.

A Glance at History in the Everglades Area

Top: Rob Storter remembered the 1910 storm when the schoolhouse was washed away. *courtesy Collier County Museums, Naples, FL.*

Middle: Broadway in Everglades City looking towards the Bank building after Hurricane Donna in 1960.

Bottom: Residents lost their belongings after Irma in 2017. *photo by the author.*

A Glance at History in the Everglades Area

DEVELOPMENT, 1950s - now

The Causeway to Chokoloskee Island was finished in 1956. Before that, children took the School Boat from the Smallwood Store. Many of the residents on Chokoloskee descend from old families. The Church of God was established in 1913 and the Smallwood Cemetery has tombs of pioneers, as does the Lopez Cemetery.

After the Smallwood Store closed in 1982, Ted's granddaughter Lynn McMillin looked for a way to preserve the premises and the memories. She formed a not-for-profit corporation to create a Museum which welcomes visitors. As she describes it, "This is not a Museum where we show history; it is where history happened."

In 1953, the Everglades National Park declared Everglades City as its Western Gateway with a Gulf Coast Ranger station on the fringe of the Ten Thousand Island. A concessionaire operates boat tours and the rangers often give talks about the flora and fauna in the park.

Plantation Island, on Halfway Creek (half way from Barron River to Turner River), was developed as a mobile home park in the early 1960s and boasts water-front access from all lots. It is a friendly community of permanent residents and week-enders.

A Glance at History in the Everglades Area

Plantation Parkway was originally Mamie Smallwood's route of the causeway to Chokoloskee but that changed when the Army Corps of Engineers built the new road. The area had been farming land where the Storters grew their sugar cane.

Everglades City has its own Planning & Zoning regulations so we can decide what our future will look like.

The Everglades Society for Historic Preservation is concerned that some of our old buildings will not be preserved, especially the Bank Building and the Depot which both date back to the County's founding.

We are also concerned about development in the surrounding area which is not within the control of the City. We fought to preserve the Smallwood Store in 2011 when it was challenged by a developer who dug up the road. And, we worry about future developments in our local area that are not within the City limits.

We rely on tourism and fishing. We live in an oasis of tranquility surrounded by preserved land.

We appreciate the independent spirit of our pioneering residents and are striving to maintain our unique historic heritage.

A Glance at History in the Everglades Area

Top: The School Boat behind the Smallwood Store took older students to Everglades City before the causeway was completed.

Bottom: In 1957 a film crew used local scenes to make the movie "Wind Across the Everglades" starring Burl Ives, Gypsy Rose Lee, and Christopher Plummer.

A Glance at History in the Everglades Area

FURTHER READING

WEBSITES

Many of the historical photos in this book come from the Florida State Archives website www.floridamemory.com.

Other photos are from the Collier County Museum archives at website www.colliermuseums.com.

To learn more about local efforts to save our unique heritage, see www.evergladeshistorical.org.

REFERENCE BOOKS

Brown, Loren G, **Totch: A Life in the Everglades,**
  1993: University Press of Florida, Gainesville, FL

Douglas, Marjory Stoneman, **Voice of the River; An Autobiography,** 1987: Pineapple Press, Sarasota, FL.

Repko, Marya, **A Brief History of the Everglades City Area,**
  2005: ECity Publishing, Everglades City, FL.

Repko, Marya, **A Brief History of the Fakahatchee,**
  2009: ECity Publishing, Everglades City, FL.

Stone, Maria, **Ochopee; the Smallest Post Office,**
  2018: ECity Publishing, Everglades City, FL.

Tebeau, Charlton W., **Florida's Last Frontier; The History of Collier County,** 1966: University of Miami Press, Miami

FICTION

Matthiessen, Peter, **Killing Mister Watson,**
  1990: Random House, New York

White, Randy Wayne, **The Man Who Invented Florida**
  1993, St. Martin's Press, New York

A Glance at History in the Everglades Area

TIMELINE

1513 Ponce de Leon claimed Florida for the Spanish
1821 United States acquired Florida from the Spanish
1845 Florida established as a state
1850 Florida granted the "swamp and overflowed" lands
1857 end of Seminole Wars
1866 end of Civil War between the states

1868 William Smith Allen settled on Potato Creek
1873 Barron Gift Collier born in Memphis, TN
1875 Harriet Bedell (later Deaconess) born in Buffalo, NY
1887 Lee County established
1889 George Storter, Jr., bought out Allen in Everglade
1890 Marjory Stoneman (later Douglas) born in Minnesota

1906 Ted Smallwood built store and appointed postmaster
1910 hurricane
1921 Barron Collier bought grapefruit farm in Deep Lake
1923 Collier County established
1926 hurricane
1928 Tamiami Trail completed
1939 Barron Collier died
1947 Everglades National Park opened

1953 Everglades incorporated as a City
1956 Chokoloskee causeway completed
1960 Hurricane Donna
1962 Collier County seat moved to Naples
1968 McLeod Park established
1989 Smallwood Store Museum opened
1998 Museum of the Everglades opened

2005 Hurricane Wilma
2017 Hurricane Irma
2020 Everglades Area Visitor Center opened

www.ingramcontent.com/pod-product-compliance
Lightning Source LLC
Chambersburg PA
CBHW052208070526
44585CB00017B/2113